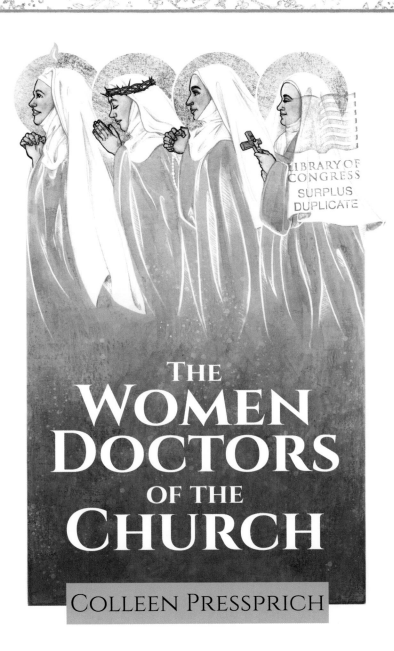

The
WOMEN
DOCTORS
OF THE
CHURCH

COLLEEN PRESSPRICH

Our Sunday Visitor
Huntington, Indiana

Library of Congress

Nihil Obstat
Msgr. Michael Heintz, Ph.D.
Censor Librorum

Imprimatur
✠ Kevin C. Rhoades
Bishop of Fort Wayne-South Bend
January 25, 2022

The *Nihil Obstat* and *Imprimatur* are official declarations that a book is free from doctrinal or moral error. It is not implied that those who have granted the *Nihil Obstat* and *Imprimatur* agree with the contents, opinions, or statements expressed.

Except where noted, the Scripture citations used in this work are taken from the *Revised Standard Version of the Bible — Second Catholic Edition* (Ignatius Edition), copyright © 1965, 1966, 2006 National Council of the Churches of Christ in the United States of America. Used by permission. All rights reserved.

Our Sunday Visitor Publishing Division
Our Sunday Visitor, Inc.
200 Noll Plaza
Huntington, IN 46750
www.osv.com
1-800-348-2440

ISBN: 978-1-68192-661-2 (Inventory No. T2567)
1. JUVENILE NONFICTION—Religiou—Christian—Biography & Autobiography.
2. SRELIGION—Christianity—Saints & Sainthood.
3. RELIGION—Christianity—Catholic.

eISBN: 978-1-68192-635-3
LCCN: 2021953281

Cover and interior design: Amanda Falk
Cover art: Adalee Hude
Interior art: Adalee Hude

PRINTED IN THE UNITED STATES OF AMERICA

For Gianna, Charlotte,

Lucy, Jane, Lily,

Margot, and Kayley.

May you become who

you were created to be

and set the world on fire.

Heaven is full of holy men and women who have lived before us. In the Catholic Church we call these people saints, and we look to them to help us know and love God better.

There is a special category of saints who are called doctors. There are thirty-seven Doctors of the Church today. Four of the Doctors of the Church are women — Saint Hildegard of Bingen, Saint Teresa of Ávila, Saint Catherine of Siena, and Saint Thérèse of Lisieux.

What does it mean for someone to be a Doctor of the Church? Are they like medical doctors, who work in a hospital and help sick people get well?

No. The men and women who are called Doctors of the Church are a different kind of doctor. They do help us get better, though! The Doctors of the Church help people to know God and his Church through their writing, their speaking, their teaching, and their lives.

The pope is the only person who can give out this title. In order to be named a Doctor of the Church, a person must meet these three requirements:

1. She must be a saint. This means that she must have lived a life of holiness and have been canonized by the Church (publicly declared to be in heaven).

2. She must understand Church teaching deeply. Doctors of the Church know the Faith, inside and out. They know what the Church teaches, and they are curious to understand why.

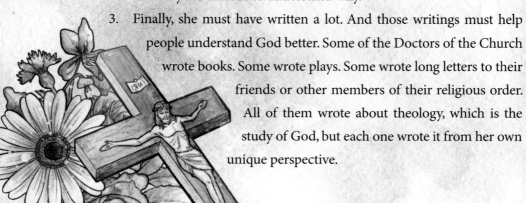

3. Finally, she must have written a lot. And those writings must help people understand God better. Some of the Doctors of the Church wrote books. Some wrote plays. Some wrote long letters to their friends or other members of their religious order. All of them wrote about theology, which is the study of God, but each one wrote it from her own unique perspective.

Hildegard, Catherine, Teresa, and Thérèse were born in different countries and at different times in history. They had different personalities, different tastes, and different ways of looking at the world. They had different strengths and different weaknesses. But they had something in common, too: They were all secure in their identity as daughters of God. Each of these women knew that she was loved deeply by her Father in heaven.

Saint Catherine of Siena once said, "When you are who God made you to be, you will set the world on fire." None of these women aspired to be a Doctor of the Church. Instead, each of them did everything she possibly could to become who God created her to be.

These four women are all unique, one of a kind. They are amazing and strong, and they fell deeply in love with Jesus. They let that love flow out of them and into the world around them. They want to help you learn more about your identity as a beloved child of God so that you can know and love him better. So that you can set the world on fire, just like they did!

Hildegard of Bingen

Born 1098 in Germany

Dare to declare who you are. It is not far from the shores of silence to the boundaries of speech. The path is not long, but the way is deep. You must not only walk there, you must be prepared to leap.

Hildegard of Bingen seemed to be able to do anything she set her mind to! What's more, she had the confidence to use the many gifts God gave her.

Hildegard was an abbess — the leader of a convent. She was wise and kind. She was a healer, a writer, a visionary, a composer, a musician, and a poet. She studied throughout her whole life and never stopped learning.

When Hildegard was three years old, she began to see visions. She called these visions her little lights from heaven. In her visions, Hildegard learned about the world that God had created. These visions helped her to be creative, energetic, and wise.

One day, when she was much older, she heard the voice of God. He told her that he wanted her to share what she had seen in her visions with

the world. Hildegard chose to be courageous. She wrote about the visions and what they meant.

Other people were very interested in what Hildegard was writing, even the pope. He thought that Hildegard's visions were true, and that she needed to tell the whole world about them. He gave her his blessing and sent her out to speak.

At this time in history, women were not often able to speak in public. Even though it was probably scary, Hildegard traveled across Europe. She went on four preaching tours, speaking to men and women about the love of God and the truth found in the Catholic Church. Hildegard always spoke boldly. She was confident in her relationship with God.

"GO FORTH INTO THE WORLD AND PROCLAIM THE GOSPEL" MK 16:15

Catherine of Siena

Born 1347 in Italy

Be who God made you to be, and
you will set the world on fire.

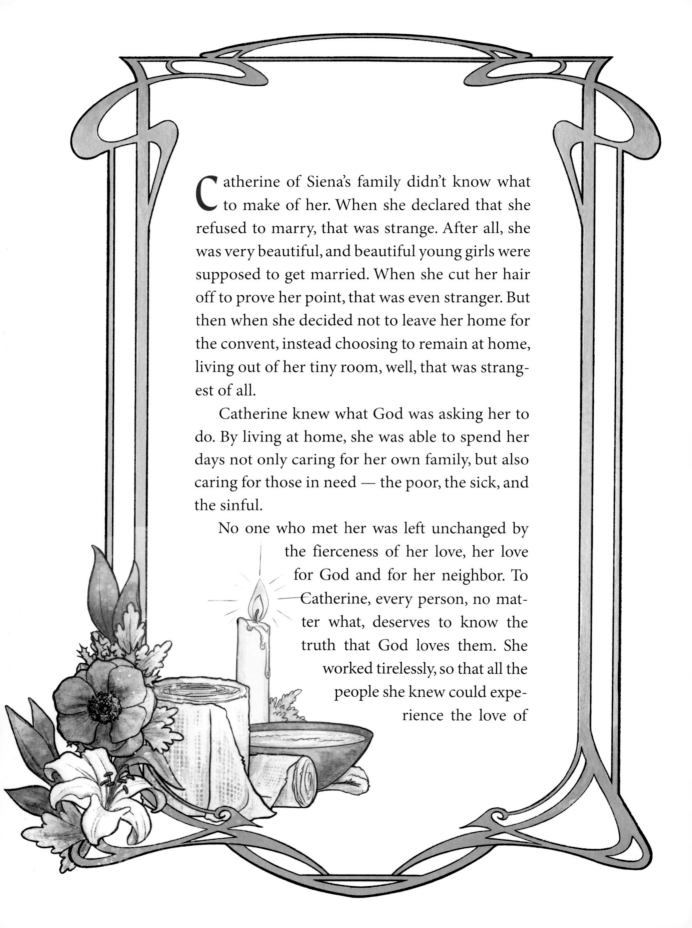

Catherine of Siena's family didn't know what to make of her. When she declared that she refused to marry, that was strange. After all, she was very beautiful, and beautiful young girls were supposed to get married. When she cut her hair off to prove her point, that was even stranger. But then when she decided not to leave her home for the convent, instead choosing to remain at home, living out of her tiny room, well, that was strangest of all.

Catherine knew what God was asking her to do. By living at home, she was able to spend her days not only caring for her own family, but also caring for those in need — the poor, the sick, and the sinful.

No one who met her was left unchanged by the fierceness of her love, her love for God and for her neighbor. To Catherine, every person, no matter what, deserves to know the truth that God loves them. She worked tirelessly, so that all the people she knew could experience the love of

God and the blessings of being a part of his Catholic Church.

Catherine lived at a time when many people had lost hope in the Catholic Church. Catherine knew that even though the Church is made up of sinners, men and women who sometimes do the wrong things and who can make terrible mistakes, that it was still Jesus' Church. She stood up to the people who were making bad choices. She even told the pope that he was wrong when he decided to live in France and persuaded him to come back to Rome. She worked hard to help the Church be the best that it could be.

Teresa of Ávila

Born 1515 in Spain

Christ has no body now on earth but yours; no hands, no feet but yours. Yours are the eyes with which Christ looks out his compassion to the world. Yours are the feet with which he is to go about doing good. Yours are the hands with which he is to bless us now.

Teresa of Ávila was beautiful, passionate, and intelligent. Her mother and father taught her about the Catholic Faith, and a relationship with Jesus came naturally to her when she was young.

As she grew up, she became distracted by the pleasure and excitement she found in society. She didn't pray as much as she used to and began to take on bad habits.

Teresa joined the Carmelite order (a religious order of women whose main focus is contemplation, community, and service) because she knew that she needed to change. But even after becoming a nun, she still kept some of her bad habits. Yet God didn't stop loving her, and he would not let his daughter get lost! He worked in her heart and began to give her special blessings when she prayed.

Soon, this spunky woman began praying more and more. She had conversations

with Jesus all the time, speaking with him as though he was her best friend, her closest companion, the person she loved the most.

She was determined to help other people get to know Jesus as well as she had. She realized the nuns in her convent (a place where religious sisters live) were not helping one another get to heaven as they ought to. She set about fixing that. Some of the sisters didn't like it, but most realized how much she loved them and wanted them to be holy. Teresa traveled all over the countryside setting up convents and helping her fellow Carmelites grow in their relationships with Jesus.

When Teresa spoke about God, people listened. She wrote to her sisters, the other women in her religious order, about how to pray, how to listen for God's voice, and how to avoid temptations. She told each of them that their souls were like a castle made from sparkling crystal, and that at the center of this castle lived the King, Jesus.

Thérèse of Lisieux

Born 1873 in France

*The splendor of the rose and the whiteness of the lily
do not rob the little violet of its scent nor the daisy
of its simple charm. If every tiny flower wanted
to be a rose, spring would lose its loveliness.*

Thérèse of Lisieux was the youngest child of a very pious family. As a little girl, she was described by her mother as spoiled, used to getting her own way.

But as she grew up, God turned her weakness into a strength — giving her such certainty of his love for her that when she prayed, she felt as though she was sitting on her heavenly Father's lap and could tell him anything.

Even when she made a mistake, did something wrong, or committed a sin, Thérèse did not hesitate to run to God. She knew that he would have mercy on her, and that she would be loved unconditionally.

Thérèse wanted more than anything to become a saint. She knew that God would not have given her that desire if he didn't want her to succeed. But sometimes she felt like there was so little that she could do! She had joined the Carmelite order like Teresa of Ávila, but she wasn't healthy or strong enough to travel and start good convents. She wanted to tell the whole world about how much Jesus loved them, but she couldn't leave her convent.

This was how Thérèse discovered

that her path to heaven was going to be different, just like she was different. She compared all the saints to flowers and decided that she would be a little wildflower which would make God smile.

Instead of being upset that she wasn't going to be asked to do big things for God like Hildegard, Catherine, Teresa, or many other saints, Thérèse was excited to have found her own path to heaven. She was going to love! She was going to love the sisters who were around her. She was going to offer prayers and make sacrifices, doing the things she very much disliked, especially for the people who made her mad or frustrated her.

She wrote about what she called her "little way." Thérèse felt like she was too weak and too small to climb the stairs to heaven herself, so she would instead climb into Jesus' arms and he would carry her there. His arms would be her elevator to heaven, getting her there quicker and more easily than the stairs. She was glad she was little!

God is not looking for saints who are exactly alike. He doesn't need another Hildegard, Catherine, Teresa, or Thérèse.

He needs you. He is looking for a saint with *your* unique strengths, weaknesses, and gifts. God wants you to use all the gifts and talents he has given you. He is looking for you to change the world by being exactly who he made you to be: his beloved child.

ABOUT THE AUTHOR

Colleen Pressprich is the author of *Marian Consecration for Families with Young Children*. She is a former missionary and Montessori teacher. She lives with her husband and children in Michigan, where she spends her time writing, homeschooling her children, and trying to find pockets of time to read. You can find more of Colleen's writing on her website, elevatortoheaven.com.

ABOUT THE ILLUSTRATOR

Wife, mom, illustrator, and Catholic author Adalee Hude is passionate about children's literature and gets giddy over good art. She spends most of the day with her very bouncy boy, evenings with her beloved Mr. H, and sneaks into Brightly Hude Studio early in the morning, with a strong cuppa tea, to draw and paint Jesus and the saints. A professional artist for half of her life now, she also enjoys singing and dancing and is on a quest to bake the perfect pie.

Helping families love and live the Catholic faith

OSV Kids is an exciting new brand on a mission to help children learn about live, and love the Catholic Faith. Every OSV Kids product is prayerfully developed to introduce children of all ages to Jesus and his Church. Using beautiful artwork, engaging storytelling, and fun activities, OSV Kids products help families form and develop their Catholic identity and learn to live the faith with great joy.

OSV Kids is a monthly magazine that delivers a fun, trustworthy, and faith-filled set of stories, images, and activities designed to help Catholic families with children ages 2-6 build up their domestic churches and live the liturgical year at home.

OSV Kids books are crafted to inspire and delight kids and parents alike. Each book is designed to kindle the Catholic imagination within young readers through creative storytelling, stunning artwork, and fidelity to the Church's teachings. With board books for infants and toddlers, picture books for young readers, and exciting stories for older kids, OSV Kids has something for everyone in your family.

Learn more at OSVKids.com